Order this book online at www.trafford.com
or email orders@trafford.com

Most Trafford titles are also available at major online book retailers.

Print information available on the last page.

ISBN: 978-1-4907-8749-7 (sc)
       978-1-4907-8748-0 (e)

Library of Congress Control Number: 2018935346

Our mission is to efficiently provide the world's finest, most comprehensive book publishing service, enabling every author to experience success. To find out how to publish your book, your way, and have it available worldwide, visit us online at www.trafford.com

Trafford rev. 06/05/2018

 www.trafford.com

North America & international
toll-free: 1 888 232 4444 (USA & Canada)
fax: 812 355 4082

Sweet Bianca
A Story About Skin Color

Sharon Hoffman

MY NAME IS BIANCA. I AM THE OLDEST OF THREE CHILDREN. I AM 6 YEARS OLD. MY YOUNGER BROTHER IS FOUR, AND MY BABY BROTHER IS ONE. I AM IN THE FIRST GRADE AT SCHOOL. I LIKE TO LEARN NEW THINGS ALL THE TIME. MY MOMMY IS A SCHOOL TEACHER, BUT NOW SHE STAYS HOME TO BE JUST A MOM TO US.

I HAVE BEEN ABLE TO DO NUMBERS AND COLORS;
SAY MY ALPHABET, AND READ BEFORE I EVER WENT
TO KINDERGARTEN. I'M NOT BETTER THAN ANYONE
ELSE, BUT I WANT TO KNOW AS MUCH AS I CAN. MY
MOM AND DAD HAVE ALWAYS MADE LEARNING
FUN FOR US.

WE DON'T WATCH T.V. LIKE OTHER KIDS DO. WE COLOR, DRAW, PLAY WORD GAMES AND MY PARENTS READ TO US ALL THE TIME. MOM AND DAD LET US WATCH SOME VIDEOS WHICH HELP US UNDERSTAND MANY THINGS.

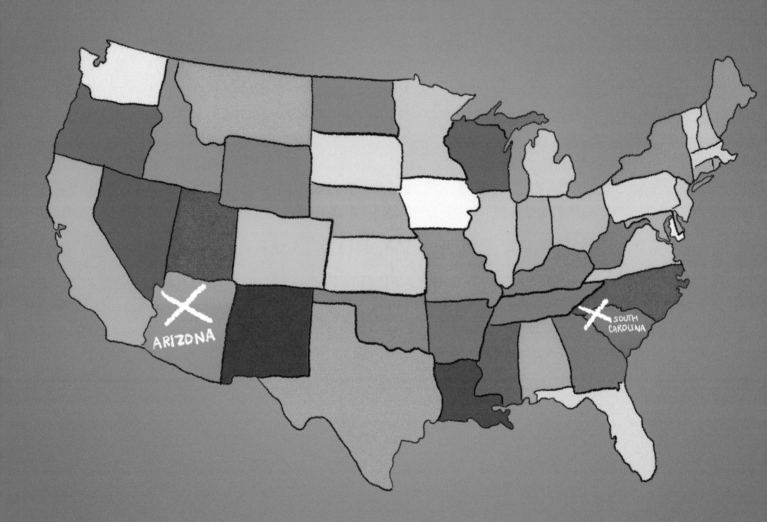

WHEN WE VISITED OUR GRAMPA AND GRAMMA, WHO LIVE FAR AWAY FROM WHERE WE LIVE, I WAS ABLE TO SOUND OUT WORDS AND READ A STORY TO MY GRAMMA.

GRAMMA TOLD ME HOW PROUD SHE WAS, AND SHE SAID THAT I COULD DO, AND BE, ANYTHING I SET MY MIND TO. I LIKED THAT BECAUSE I THINK I CAN DO LOTS OF THINGS ALREADY AND IT WAS NICE TO HEAR THAT SHE BELIEVED IN ME.

WHEN I BEGAN GOING TO FIRST GRADE, I HAD TO RIDE A SCHOOL BUS WHICH WOULD PICK ME UP AT MY HOUSE, AND TAKE ME TO SCHOOL. AFTER SCHOOL, THE BUS WOULD TAKE ME RIGHT BACK HOME, WHERE WE STARTED FROM, THAT MORNING.

I LIKE ALL THE OTHER KIDS, AND I AM NOT SHY OR AFRAID TO TALK TO ANY OF THEM. I WANT THEM TO BE MY FRIENDS, AND I WANT TO BE THEIR FRIEND TOO.

ONE DAY, THE BUS PICKED ME UP, AND ON THE WAY TO SCHOOL A NEW BOY WAS RIDING THE BUS FOR THE FIRST TIME. HE HAD JUST MOVED HERE AND SAT IN THE SEAT BEHIND ME. HE KEPT KICKING THE BACK OF THE SEAT, AND WHEN I ASKED HIM TO STOP, HE SPIT IN MY HAIR.

I WAS SCARED, AND STARTED TO CRY. HE CALLED ME NAMES AND I DIDN'T KNOW WHY HE WOULD DO THAT. I DIDN'T DO ANYTHING TO HIM. I JUST GOT ON THE BUS AS USUAL, AND SAT IN MY SEAT AS I ALWAYS DID, WHEN HE STARTED TO ACT BAD TO ME. WHEN WE ARRIVED AT SCHOOL, I TOLD THE TEACHER WHAT HAPPENED, AND SHE JUST TOLD ME TO SIT DOWN.

I DID, AND WAS WAITING FOR HER TO SAY SOMETHING TO THE BOY. SHE DIDN'T. ALL MORNING I SAT IN CLASS BUT NOTHING HAPPENED TO THE BOY AND WHEN IT FINALLY WAS TIME TO GO HOME, HE SAT BEHIND ME AGAIN, AND DID THE SAME THINGS ALL THE WAY.

WHEN THE BUS STOPPED AT MY HOUSE, I RAN IN AND TOLD MY MOM WHAT HAD HAPPENED. WE HAD TO WASH MY HAIR, AND IT TAKES A LOT OF TIME TO WASH AND DRY BECAUSE IT IS VERY LONG AND CURLY.

WHEN MY DAD CAME HOME FROM WORK AND HEARD WHAT HAD HAPPENED, HE AND MY MOM SAT ME DOWN AND TRIED TO EXPLAIN WHY SOME PEOPLE ARE MEAN AND HATEFUL.

LATER, MY DAD WENT TO THE SCHOOL AND TALKED TO THE PRINCIPAL ABOUT WHAT HAD HAPPENED. I GUESS THE PRINCIPAL TALKED TO THE TEACHER AND THE BOY'S PARENTS, BECAUSE AFTER ABOUT A WEEK, THE BOY STOPPED BEING MEAN, AND SAT IN ANOTHER SEAT.

I WANTED TO TELL YOU WHAT HAPPENED TO ME, IN CASE SOMETHING LIKE THIS EVER HAPPENS TO YOU. I DIDN'T UNDERSTAND WHY THE BOY DID WHAT HE DID, BUT MY PARENTS DID THEIR BEST TO EXPLAIN IT TO ME THIS WAY: MY DAD HAS LIGHT SKIN, HAIR, AND BLUE EYES. HE IS CALLED "WHITE". MY MOM HAS DARKER SKIN, HAIR, AND EYES. SHE CAME FROM MEXICO.

THERE ARE MANY DIFFERENT COLORS OF SKIN, HAIR, AND EYES. THERE IS BLACK, YELLOW, WHITE, BROWN, AND REDDISH SKIN. THERE ARE BLUE, GREEN, BROWN, AND HAZEL EYES; SOMETIMES ONE BLUE AND ONE BROWN EYE. THERE ARE EVEN PEOPLE WITH PINK EYES.

MY DAD AND MOM TELL ME THAT I AM A GREAT BLEND OF BOTH OF THEM. I AM DARKER THAN MY DAD AND LOOK MORE LIKE MY MOM. MY YOUNGER BROTHER IS LIGHT, LIKE MY DAD, AND HAS BLUE EYES TOO. MY BABY BROTHER IS DARKER THAN MY DAD, BUT LIGHTER THAN MY MOM. WE ARE ALL THE SAME FAMILY EACH HAS HIS OR HER OWN SPECIAL DIFFERENCE. THE WORLD WOULD LOOK PRETTY FUNNY IF WE WERE ALL ALIKE, BUT OUR DIFFERENCES SHOULDN'T MAKE OTHER PEOPLE TREAT US MEAN AND HATEFUL. GOD MADE EACH ONE OF US IN HIS OWN LIKENESS: SO IF WE ALL LOOK DIFFERENT – GOD MUST LOOK LIKE ALL OF US BLENDED TOGETHER – LIKE HE BLENDED THE COLORS OF THE RAINBOWS.

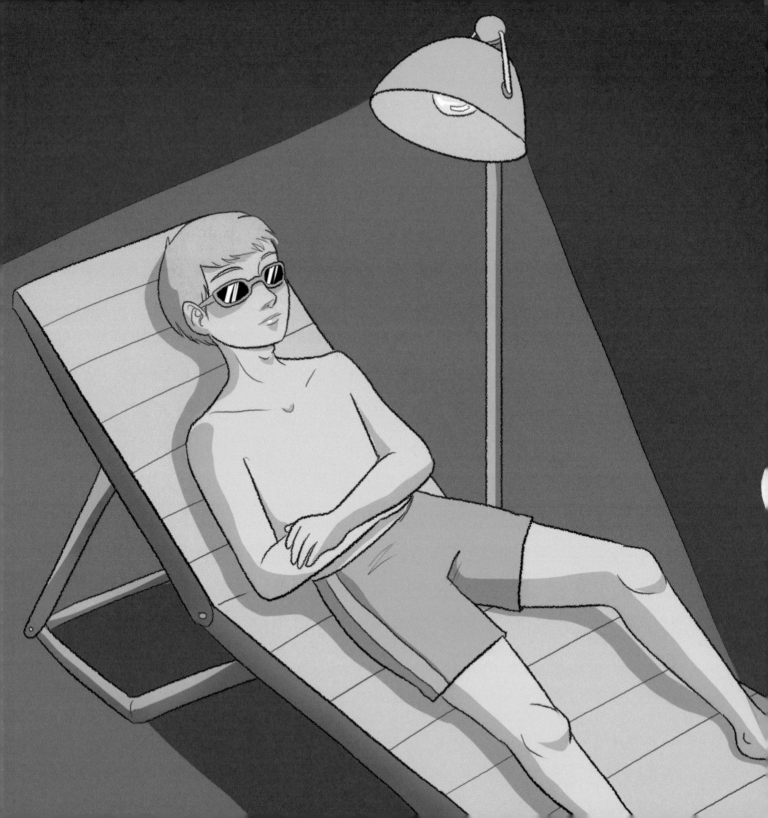

PEOPLE HAVE A LOT OF DIFFERENT HAIR COLORS ALSO. RED, YELLOW, BROWN, BLACK, GREY, WHITE, AND I HAVE EVEN SEEN BLUE AND GREEN HAIR. BUT THAT WASN'T WHAT THEY WERE BORN WITH. THEY HAVE COLOR IN BOTTLES THAT PEOPLE PUT ON THEIR HAIR TO MAKE A DIFFERENT COLOR THAT THEY MAY LIKE BETTER. PEOPLE EVEN HAVE NO HAIR. IT IS HARD TO CHANGE THE COLOR OF YOUR SKIN. SOME PEOPLE SIT IN THE SUNSHINE TO CHANGE FROM WHITE TO BROWN. THEY MOSTLY GET 'RED' AND THEN SOMETIMES IT PEELS OFF BECAUSE IT WASN'T A 'REAL' COLOR AND IT TURNS BACK TO WHAT IT STARTED AS.

MY GRAMMA TOLD ME THAT WE SHOULD TREAT PEOPLE AS IF WE COULDN'T SEE THEM AT ALL.

THEN THEIR DIFFERENCES WOULDN'T SHOW AND WE WOULD LIKE THEM OR NOT LIKE THEM, FOR THE WAY THEY ACTED AND NOT THE WAY THEY LOOKED. THE COLOR OF A PERSON'S SKIN IS **WHAT** THEY ARE; NOT **WHO** THEY ARE.

IF YOU NEVER TASTED AN ORANGE BECAUSE YOU DIDN'T LIKE THE COLOR, YOU WOULD NEVER KNOW HOW **SWEET** IT COULD TASTE!!!

Printed in the United States
By Bookmasters